SAMMY SOSA

SAMMY SOSA

HOME RUN HERO

Jeff Savage

LERNER
SPORTS
A DIVISION OF LERNER PUBLISHING GROUP

To Steven Gaab, Super Slugger

First Avenue Editions
An imprint of Lerner Publishing Group
241 First Avenue North
Minneapolis, Minnesota 55401 U.S.A.

Website address: www.lernerbooks.com

Library of Congress Cataloging-in-Publication Data

Savage, Jeff, 1961–
    Sammy Sosa, home run hero / Jeff Savage.
        p.   cm.
Includes bibliographical references and index.
Summary: A biography of the Chicago Cubs outfielder known for hitting many home runs and doing humanitarian work in his native country, the Dominican Republic.
    ISBN 0–8225–9858–2 (pbk. : alk. paper)
    1. Sosa, Sammy, 1968–   —Juvenile literature. 2. Baseball players—Dominican Republic—Biography—Juvenile literature. I. Title: Sammy Sosa. II. Title.
    GV865.S59 S69   1999
    796.357'092—dc21
                                                            99–050482

Manufactured in the United States of America
2 3 4 5 6 7 – JR – 07 06 05 04 03 02

Contents

Slammin' Sammy

Sammy Sosa crossed the chalk line on the ball field and headed to rightfield, smiling. The largest crowd of the year had packed Wrigley Field in Chicago on this warm September Sunday to see if the Chicago Cubs outfielder would hit a home run.

Five days earlier in St. Louis, Sammy's friend and rival had made history. St. Louis's Mark McGwire had broken the most glamorous record in sports—the single-season home run record. Babe Ruth's record of 60 home runs had lasted 34 years until Roger Maris broke it in 1961. Maris's mark of 61 homers stood for 37 years until McGwire hit a line drive over the leftfield fence for number 62. Sammy raced in from the outfield to hug McGwire near home plate. "Don't get too far ahead," Sammy told McGwire. "Wait for me." At the time, Sammy had 58 homers of his own.

But by this day, Sammy was up to 60 home runs. Young men with painted letters on bare chests stood side-by-side spelling S-A-M-M-Y and S-O-S-A. Thousands gathered in the streets outside the stadium in case Sammy hit one that far. "Sammy is an idol," said Cubs teammate Mark Grace. "He is absolutely adored in Chicago."

Sammy is also a hero in the Dominican Republic, the tiny Caribbean island nation where he grew up. His name and likeness appear everywhere. On the dusty streets of his hometown of San Pedro de Macoris, barefoot children dressed in rags play baseball with an orange and pretend to be him. Sammy understands. "When I was young," he said, "I was dreaming that I would be here in America. Now that I am here, every day is like a holiday for me. Every time I wake up, I say, 'God Bless America.' "

In Latino neighborhoods in the United States, fans paint Sammy's name in blue on street curbs and in white polish or soap on car windshields. Omar Minaya, a major league scout, discovered Sammy.

One of Sammy's fans in Washington Heights, New York, painted his car to celebrate Sammy's feats.

Minaya, who signed him to a baseball contract 13 years earlier, said: "He's given so much hope to so many people of all races and economic backgrounds, but especially to people in poor Third World countries. He's shown that with hard work, you can make it. And make it with class."

Sammy is a hero to people of all races. As he says, "No matter who we are or where we come from, we are one person." He is a gentle person of humility and grace. He loves everyone, and it is easy to love him. From the bleachers, fans yell for him. The hundreds of underprivileged kids whose tickets he buys as part of his Sammy Sundays program, join the chants of "Sam-eee! Sam-eee!" that echo through the stadium whenever he is up to bat.

The chants started up again for Sammy in the fifth inning as he strode to the plate with his two-pound bat. He had flied out and drawn an **intentional walk** his first two times up. With a Cubs runner at first base, there was no chance for Milwaukee Brewers pitcher Bronswell Patrick to walk Sammy on purpose again.

The outfielders stood deep, nearly on the warning track, as Patrick fired a pitch. Sammy let it go by for a strike. Patrick delivered again, and this time Sammy swung. Boom! The ball soared like a rocket to left. Sammy hopped sideways over the plate, like he always does when he knows he's hit a homer. The ball flew over the bleachers and out onto Waveland Avenue. Sammy circled the bases pumping his fist. The ball smacked the pavement 480 feet from home plate and bounced down the street with hundreds of fans giving chase.

Sammy starts his home run trot with a sideways jump.

A man watching the game on a portable television jumped from his van to find the ball at his feet. He sold it after the game for $10,000 to another man who gave the ball to Sammy, just so he could meet him.

Sammy touched home plate and gave his trade-mark thump-kiss salute. He thumped his heart with his fist, then kissed his fingers twice. The first kiss was for his mother, the second for his friends in the Dominican Republic and the fans of Chicago. He sat down in the dugout and doused his face with water. With the fans shouting themselves hoarse, and his teammates urging him, he stepped out to take a bow.

Sammy's two-run homer gave his team an 8–3 lead. With two weeks left in the season, the Cubs were locked in a battle for the wild-card berth in the National League playoffs with the New York Mets and San Francisco Giants. "I don't want the record. I want to be in the playoffs," Sammy had said. "I'd love if it's going to happen, but if it happens to Mark McGwire, I love Mark McGwire. The whole world knows that. For myself, whatever happens from now on is a gift. I have another idea and another goal—to go to the playoffs. I like that much better."

But the Chicago **bullpen** could not hold the lead.

The Cubs trailed 10-8 in the bottom of the ninth inning when Sammy came to the plate again. With the bases empty and the fans on their tiptoes, Sammy worked the **count** to two balls and one strike and then blasted Eric Plunk's next pitch deep to left. It sailed high and deep and out of the park, landing 480 feet away onto the street again. Hundreds of fans chased it up an alley. When a man emerged from a wild scramble holding the ball, police officers whisked him to the nearest station for his own protection. Sammy gave his thump-kiss salute at home plate and mouthed the words "I love you, Mama," before being swallowed up by teammates.

Meanwhile, six miles away, Sonia Sosa, Sammy's wife, was rushing out the door of their apartment.

Fans wave the flag of the Dominican Republic.

She had been sitting under a hair dryer, watching the game on television when Sammy smashed number 62. "I jumped up and said, 'Oh, man, I've got to get to the ballpark,'" said Sonia. She yanked the curlers from her hair, told the housekeeper to watch the four young Sosa children, and raced downstairs to a taxi cab. "Please hurry," she told the cab driver. "I want to see my husband." The driver said, "Don't worry. I'll get you there."

While Chicago fans gave Sammy a loud, long cheer that carried on for six minutes, thousands of people flooded the streets of the Dominican Republic. They clanged pots and pans and shouted "Sammy, querido!" *Sammy, loved one!* In Latino communities throughout the United States, car horns blared, and kids pedaled bicycles towing strings of cans and cried his name. The fans at Wrigley finally calmed down but revved up again a moment later when the Cubs rallied to tie the game. Then, in the 10th inning, Mark Grace homered for the Cubs' victory.

Sammy was the first to greet his teammate at home plate, and his bear hug was so strong that Grace screamed, "Sammy, let go!" Cubs catchers Tyler Houston and Scott Servais hoisted Sammy onto their shoulders as cheers rained down.

Sammy's teammates carry him off the field after his two home runs led the Cubs over the Brewers.

Little boys in the Dominican Republic play baseball just the way Sammy did 20 years ago.

16

Learning the Game

Sammy Sosa is rich. He owns three homes, a dozen cars, a 60-foot yacht, and a $42.5-million contract that runs until 2002. But Sammy did not grow up rich.

Samuel Peralta Sosa was born November 12, 1968, the fifth of seven children born to Juan and Lucrecya Sosa. Sammy grew up in the bustling port town of San Pedro de Macoris in the Dominican Republic. The countries of the Dominican Republic and Haiti share the island of Hispaniola 600 miles from Florida. Most of the nearly 10 million people in the Dominican Republic work in the sugar cane fields or in the factories for low wages.

Sammy lived in a poor neighborhood called Barrio Mexico, in a two-room unit of an abandoned hospital. Sammy shared his room with his four brothers and two sisters. They slept on foam pads on the floor. Sammy's brothers and sisters affectionately called him *Mayki.*

Sammy's father worked in the sugar cane fields and repaired roads. His mother sold food on the streets and at the factories. Together they barely made enough money to feed their children. Sammy was seven years old when his father died suddenly of a stroke. Sammy and his brothers and sisters had to take jobs to help the family survive. Sammy shined shoes and sold fruit on the street. His mother came home in the evenings with enough money for them to eat their first meal of the day. She ached from walking all day, and Sammy would massage her feet. Sammy quit school in the eighth grade to work full time to help his family eat. He sold fruit and washed cars during the day and worked as a janitor in a shoe factory at night.

Sammy's first love was boxing. He and his friends taped sponges to their fists and sparred. Sammy's mother did not like to see him get hit. "He would tell me not to worry, that it was nothing," Lucrecya said.

"I would tell him, 'My son, for a mother it is a lot.'"
Sammy had a speech problem, and sometimes his
friends teased him and called him "Gago," which
means *stutterer.* When Sammy's fists suddenly
started flying for real, the teasing would stop.

When he was 13, his older brother, Juan, con-
vinced him to quit boxing and try baseball. Sammy
used a tree branch for a bat, a bundle of socks for a
ball, and a cardboard milk carton for a glove. "I
would cut the bottom off the carton and stick my
hand inside," he said. "Then I would tear holes for
my fingers." Sammy fell in love with baseball.

One of the favorite sports in the Dominican
Republic—and in all of Latin America—is baseball.
There, people play the game on dirt fields with splin-
tered bats and worn hardballs, and on streets with
broomsticks and oranges. Some of the players are
lucky enough to be seen by major league scouts
and signed to contracts. Juan Marichal, known as
the Dominican Dandy, pitched for the San Francisco
Giants. He is in the Baseball Hall of Fame.

The best Latin-born major leaguer ever was
Roberto Clemente from nearby Puerto Rico. Sammy
would later wear the number 21 on his Cubs uni-
form to honor Clemente. The Pittsburgh slugger died

in a plane crash while delivering food supplies to Nicaragua after an earthquake ravaged that Central American country.

Sammy saw Dominican baseball stars like George Bell of the Blue Jays, Joaquin Andujar of the Astros, and Pedro Guerrero of the Dodgers when they returned home in the off-season. Sammy even shined their shoes. He saw their gold chains and their fancy cars.

"People would come up to them, and they were always in the middle of a crowd," Sammy said. "They lived in beautiful houses. I can remember thinking it would be nice to live like that."

One day a man approached Sammy with something under his arm. The man was Bill Chase, an American who owned a factory in the Dominican Republic. Chase had met Sammy and his brothers several months earlier and liked them. Chase returned from a business trip to the United States with a present for Sammy—a baseball glove.

Soon afterward, Sammy met Hector Peguero, a baseball instructor who taught kids the fundamentals of the game for 67 cents a week. Sometimes the kids could afford to pay and sometimes they couldn't. Peguero saw Sammy playing baseball one day.

Roberto Clemente was an All-Star outfielder for the Pittsburgh Pirates from 1954 to 1972.

He noticed Sammy was skinny, but that he had big hands and wide shoulders, and that he swung very hard. Peguero offered to give Sammy a few pointers.

Sammy's older brother, Luis, noticed Sammy's improvement. He told Peguero, "I will work my fruit stand fulltime so Mayki doesn't have to shine shoes and wash cars all day. You teach him to play ball." Sammy began to work with Peguero as much as six hours a day at a dirt field near a prison.

They worked mostly on batting. To prevent Sammy's front foot from springing forward too soon, Peguero tied a rope around it and held it in place until the last instant. To keep Sammy's back foot from stepping, Peguero placed a ball in front of it, then a bat, and finally, when that didn't work, a broken bottle. Because Sammy was too slow to be a singles hitter, Peguero would tell him to "swing big and hard." Sometimes Sammy's swing was so wild, with his head flailing about, that Peguero had to stand behind him and hold his head in place.

On rainy days, Peguero pitched to Sammy in his tiny apartment. They used kernels of corn and bottle caps for balls. On sunny days, Peguero pitched hundreds of balls to him in the dirt field. Sammy swung and swung until the sun went down, but he never wanted to stop. "Mas [more]!" he yelled. After a grueling workout one evening, Sammy went into a restaurant. The owner sniffed and said, "You smell too bad to come in here." Sammy replied, "That bad smell will be worth a lot of money one day."

Each month Sammy hit the ball a bit farther. He and his coach had to extend the field every so often by hacking off the dry grass with a big knife. Finally the field stretched clear to the prison wall. When Sammy hit a ball so far that it sailed over the wall and through a building window, they both knew he was good enough to try organized baseball.

Sammy joined a local Little League team and soon a major league scout spotted him. Amado Dinzey of the Texas Rangers had been combing the Dominican Republic for young talent when he saw Sammy in a game. Sammy's quick bat and strong arm impressed Dinzey, and he called Rangers head scout Omar Minaya to come down and take a look.

Minaya flew to the Dominican Republic and arranged for Sammy to take a four-hour bus ride to Puerto Plata to meet him. When Sammy stepped off the bus, Minaya could hardly believe his eyes. Sammy wore a ratty Philadelphia Phillies jersey, torn blue jeans, and baseball shoes with holes in them. He stood about 5 feet, 10 inches tall, which was a nice height for a 16-year-old, but he weighed no more than 140 pounds. This bean pole was the kid Minaya had come to the island to see? "He looked weak and malnourished," Minaya recalled. "Some of the balls he hit to the outfield would run out of steam, and to me, that was malnourishment."

But Minaya noticed something else about Sammy. "He got off that bus ready to hit," said the scout. "I sensed something inside him, a kind of fire. Right from the start, you could see how aggressive he was. His time in the 60-yard-dash was 7.5 [seconds], well below average. But he could throw, and the ball would just jump off his bat."

Rangers officials returned with Sammy to his home in San Pedro de Macoris to discuss a minor-league contract. They offered him $3,000 to sign but Sammy asked for $4,000. They agreed on $3,500. Sammy felt rich! He proudly gave the money to his mother, keeping just a few dollars for himself to buy his first bicycle.

Early the next year, Sammy was at the local airport hugging his family goodbye. He was going to start the 1986 season with the Rangers' rookie-league team in Sarasota, Florida. He knew only a few words of English. His mother worried about how he would manage in a new country with new people and a new language. As Sammy headed for the plane, he looked back to see his mother crying.

Sammy's mother watches her famous son play baseball on television in a grand house that he built for her.

Sammy broke into the big leagues with the Texas Rangers but soon became a Chicago White Sox.

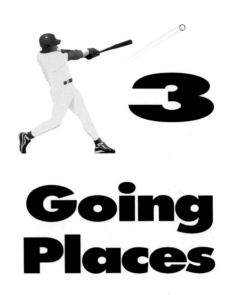

3

Going Places

Lucrecya Sosa had nothing to fear. Sammy listened closely to his coaches and asked lots of questions. He ordered at fast-food restaurants by repeating the words of the person in front of him. And he made friends. "It was hard for me because my English was not the way it is now," he said. "I got lucky because there were some Puerto Rican players who I hung out with, and they helped me out a lot."

Sammy had a fine rookie season, with a **batting average** of .275 and 19 doubles and 96 total bases—which led the Gulf Coast League. He hit just four homers, however. He improved to 11 homers a year later with Class A Gastonia of the South

Atlantic League, and he led the team with a .279 average, 145 hits, 27 doubles, and 73 runs scored.

But Sammy struggled to learn the game's basic strategies, like moving runners over with a **sacrifice bunt** or hitting the **cutoff** on outfield throws. He often made his coaches angry by trying to do too much. But they couldn't stay mad at him for long. His jovial and generous personality endeared him to his teammates and coaches. "He always had a smile and a glow in his eyes," said Rangers scouting director Sandy Johnson. "And he was hungry for success."

Each off-season, Sammy worked on his speed by running long distances and sprints back home. At Port Charlotte of the Florida State League in 1988, he displayed his new swiftness, setting a Class A record with 12 triples and stealing a career-high 42 bases. When he hit .297 with seven homers the first two months of 1989 at Class AA Tulsa, the Rangers called him up to the major league team. "It was the happiest day of my life," Sammy said.

The following day, Sammy made his debut in Arlington, Texas, as his team's rightfielder. He rapped a single off New York Yankees pitcher Andy Hawkins for his first big-league hit, then ripped a double later in the game. Five nights later, he drilled a rocket off Boston Red Sox ace Roger Clemens for his first home run. "From that day," said Sammy, "I said to myself, 'I think I'll be a good player.'"

As a 20-year-old rookie surrounded by big-league veterans, Sammy had plenty to learn, and he sought the advice of a fellow Dominican. "The player who I hung around with who taught me a lot was Julio Franco," Sammy said. "He was with the Texas Rangers when I was there. When I was a rookie, he showed me the way to survive in the major leagues." Sammy was so eager that too often he swung at bad pitches and tried to hit every ball to the moon. With his average down to .238 on July 20, Sammy was sent back down to the minor leagues.

At Class AAA Oklahoma City, he did all he could to earn his way back. He was the first to show up at the field each day and the last to leave. When the Chicago White Sox Class AAA team from Vancouver, Canada, came to Oklahoma City for four games, Sox general manager Larry Himes came with them. Himes was glad he did. After each day's game beneath the broiling sun had ended, Himes watched a young man from the other team return to the field. The young ballplayer would carry a bag of balls and a batting tee and roll a batting screen. The kid, Sammy, would stand in the hot, humid air and whack ball after ball off the tee into the screen. "He didn't know we were there," said Himes. "When everyone else went inside to cool off, he would stay out in the heat. We thought it was a one-day thing, but he did it every day. He just had great desire and drive to make himself better."

Himes traded veteran hitter Harold Baines for Sammy the next day. Himes had to talk White Sox owner Jerry Reinsdorf into the deal. The Rangers agreed only because they were seven games out of first place and hoped Baines would help them to the top. Texas finished the season in fourth place, 16 games back.

Meanwhile, Sammy went to the Vancouver team for two weeks and then was called up to the White Sox where he joined his new team in Minnesota. In his debut that night, he went 3-for-3 with a home run, two runs scored, two **runs batted in,** and a stolen base. He played in 33 games, batting **leadoff** most of the time, and finished with a .273 average and three home runs. The White Sox signed him to a contract for $500,000.

Sammy was rich! He bought a house for his mother, a hair salon and boutique for his sisters, and fancy cars for his brothers. He bought big jewelry for his neck and wrists and put gel in his hair.

Sammy's first full year in the majors in 1990 was a success from the start. He batted leadoff and cracked a home run to open the game four times! He blasted 15 home runs in the season and also rapped out 26 doubles and 10 triples. He drove in 70 runs.

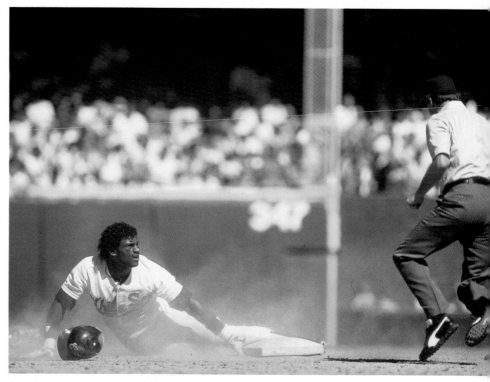

In 1990, his first full year in the majors, Sammy stole 32 bases for the Chicago White Sox.

He even stole 32 bases. He was the only player in the American League to reach double figures in doubles, triples, and homers. The last player to accomplish the feat was Harold Baines.

But Sammy was still impatient at the plate. He swung at too many bad pitches. He batted just .233 and struck out 150 times. "I became a professional ballplayer with a lot of talent and no discipline at home plate," he said, "because I didn't have time to play when I was a boy." Sammy returned home to San Pedro de Macoris and practiced his hitting.

One night at a dance club, Sammy met Sonia, who would become his wife. She was working as a dancer for a TV variety show in the Dominican Republic. Sammy asked a waiter to deliver her a note. "If you will do me the honor of having one dance with me," he wrote, "it will be the start of a beautiful friendship." They danced, and then Sammy gave her tickets to a winter-league ballgame.

"I didn't know he was a ballplayer," Sonia said. "I thought he was just another traveling salesman in gold chains." Sammy and Sonia developed a friendship and fell in love. "Every time I saw him," Sonia said, "I felt electricity from the tips of my toes right to my heart." They married a year later.

*With free-swinging Sammy at the plate, the White Sox
didn't know whether to expect a strikeout or a home run.*

Sammy and his wife, Sonia, met at a dance club in the Dominican Republic.

Sammy blasted two home runs and drove in five runs against the Orioles on Opening Day 1991 in Baltimore. He struggled the rest of the season and went to the minors for a month. He had trouble hitting an outside curveball. The White Sox coaches grew impatient. Sammy sensed it. He pressed harder. "I was trying to hit two home runs in every **at bat,"** he said. He finished the season with only 10 home runs and 33 runs batted in. He batted just .203. Only one player in the American League had a lower average—Mark McGwire of the Oakland A's.

Sammy was just 22 years old, but the White Sox gave up on him. Larry Himes didn't. The Sox general manager had been fired by owner Jerry Reinsdorf after the season and had taken a job with the Chicago Cubs. On the eve of the 1992 season opener, Himes traded slugger George Bell to the Sox for Sammy.

Sox fans laughed and said Himes was making the same mistake again. But Himes believed in the kid with the rough skills and the big heart. Sammy was thrilled to be a Cub. "Larry," he said, "I feel like I am out of jail. I will never let you down."

Sammy hit just 10 home runs in 1991.

Swinging for the Fences

The Chicago Cubs had not won the World Series since 1908. Sammy wanted to help change that. He weighed just 165 pounds, but he immediately started a conditioning and nutrition program. He wanted more power so he could hit home runs.

In the season's first month, Sammy hit just .211. He drove in a run on Opening Day 1992 and didn't knock in another for three weeks. He finally broke the drought on May 5 with his second run batted in. Two days later he popped his first home run off Houston Astros pitcher Ryan Bowen. He began to gain confidence, and by late May he had raised his average 40 points. On June 10 at Busch Stadium in

St. Louis, he blasted two homers. The following night in Montreal, Expos pitcher Dennis Martinez threw a pitch that hit Sammy and broke his hand. Doctors fused the bone back together and put Sammy's hand in a cast. He had to sit on the bench for six weeks.

At last his hand healed, and on July 27 he got back in the lineup. In his first game back, in his first at bat, on the first pitch from Pittsburgh Pirates pitcher Doug Drabek, Sammy crushed a towering home run. He hit two more homers that week.

Dominican coach Hector Peguero came for a visit. Sammy took Peguero into the locker room to meet his Cubs teammates. "This is Hector Peguero," Sammy told everyone. "The man who taught me to play baseball." In the game that day, Peguero watched Sammy score from first base on a **pitchout** by stealing second base and dashing home on a bad throw by the catcher.

In his first nine games off the disabled list, Sammy hit .385 with three homers and nine runs batted in. But in the 10th game, Sammy fouled a pitch off his left ankle. He collapsed in pain. His ankle was broken. Doctors operated and put his foot in a cast. Sammy missed the rest of the season.

Sammy returned to Chicago the next spring with 20 pounds of muscle added to his frame. His hard work paid off. In a game in May at Colorado, he went 5-for-6 with two homers and five runs batted in. In a game in June at San Diego, he smacked two more homers, giving him 16 for the season, breaking his career high. In a game in July at Colorado, he went 6-for-6 to become the first Cub ever to get six hits in a game. Combined with his three hits the day earlier, his nine consecutive hits broke another team record.

In a game in September at Los Angeles, he stole four bases to tie another Chicago record. He hit his 30th homer September 2 off New York Mets pitcher Josias Manzanillo. He stole his 30th base September 15 against the San Francisco Giants.

Sammy became the first player in Cubs history to have 30 or more home runs and 30 or more stolen bases in one season. He finished the 1993 season with 33 homers and 36 steals.

Sammy bought a gold necklace with a large medallion of two crossed bats and the numbers 30-30. He wore it to the park each day, but he had to hide it in a safe before games because it was too big to wear on the field. Teammate Mark Grace said, "No way he could run with that on." Pitcher Rod Beck said, "That wasn't a chain. It was a license plate." Sammy even changed his car license plate to *SS 30 30.* Later he built a shopping mall in San Pedro de Macoris at the spot where he used to shine shoes and named it 30-30 Plaza. In front of the mall is a huge water fountain. All the coins tossed into the pool go to the local shoeshine boys. During the off-season, Sammy stands at the fountain and passes out money to everyone who comes by.

In 1994, Sammy batted a career-high .300 with 25 homers and 70 RBIs. He also led the team with 22 steals. His average dipped to .268 the following year, but his homers climbed to 36, his RBIs to 119, and his steals to 34. He played in his first All-Star Game midway through the 1995 season.

"Without America, I don't know where I'd be," said Sammy. "Whatever happened to me, I don't know how to explain it to you." He said that he practiced baseball every day in the off-season.

On May 16, 1996, Sammy became the first Cubs player in history to hit two homers in the same inning. He led off the seventh inning with a bomb off Houston Astros pitcher Jeff Tabaka, then smacked a two-run shot off Jim Dougherty.

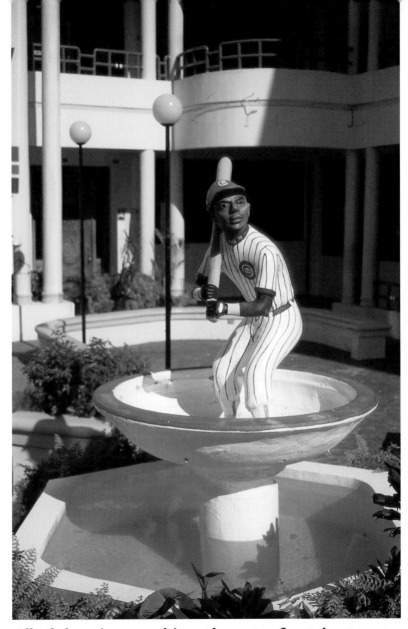

All of the coins tossed into the water fountain at Sammy's 30-30 Plaza in San Pedro de Macoris go to the local shoeshine boys.

Sammy's speed on the basepaths enabled him to steal 22 bases during the 1997 season.

Two weeks later, Sammy hit three homers in a game against the Philadelphia Phillies. He had become one of the most feared sluggers in baseball.

On August 20 at Wrigley Field, Sammy was leading the league in home runs with 40 when he faced Florida Marlins pitcher Mark Hutton. The bases were loaded. Would Sammy hit his first **grand slam?** Hutton fired a pitch inside. The ball cracked Sammy on the hand and shattered a bone. The bone was broken in so many places that surgeons had to remove it from Sammy's hand in little pieces.

Sammy's hand mended over the winter, and he was back at spring training in 1997. Midway through the season, Sammy signed a four-year contract with the Cubs for $42 million. *Forty-two million!* Sammy barely knew how much money that was. Right away, he had a bigger home built for his mother. He had a baseball complex built for youth teams in San Pedro de Macoris. He bought ambulances for many hospitals in the Dominican Republic. He bought 2,500 computers for the Dominican Republic school system.

Sammy stayed healthy throughout 1997 and was one of just four players in baseball to play in all 162 games. He finished with 36 homers and tied his career high with 119 runs batted in. But he struck out 174 times, highest in the league. Some Cubs fans called him "Sammy So-So." That bothered Sammy. Even worse, the Cubs had started the season with 14 straight losses and wound up in last place in their division. Sammy wondered if his team would ever make the playoffs.

Forty home runs and forty million dollars would satisfy most stars, but not Sammy. He wanted to do more. He decided to rework his swing. Back home in the Dominican Republic, he studied videotapes of three batters: teammate Mark Grace, Atlanta Braves third baseman Chipper Jones, and himself. All three started their swing by tapping their front foot. Sammy noticed that Grace and Jones started their tap-step when the pitch was halfway to the plate. Sammy started his when the ball was just a few feet from him, which made him hurry his swing. He practiced tapping sooner. He lowered his hands about six inches, like slugger Barry Bonds. This way, he could swing faster, which meant he would have more time to decide whether to swing.

"Sammy Claus" made lots of people happy.

Sammy hit hundreds of balls each day at a park in San Pedro de Macoris. He took time out in December for a "Sammy Claus" tour. On the tour, Sammy gave thousands of gifts to children in schools and hospitals in the Dominican Republic and in Chicago, Philadelphia, New York, Miami, and Washington, D.C. The rest of the time, he practiced his new swing.

Sammy changed something else, too. He took off his rings and necklaces, even his 30-30 medallion, and put them in a dresser drawer. The only piece of jewelry he wanted was a championship ring.

The Great Home Run Race

The first sign that Sammy was a different hitter in 1998 came on April 4 when he blasted his first home run of the year. "The only real mistake I made," said Montreal Expos pitcher Marc Valdes, "was throwing a pitch up and away to Sosa. Normally he tries to pull a ball like that. Today he went with the pitch."

Sammy smacked six homers in April and kept cool about it. "Right now I'm just trying to calm down and relax and watch the ball a little bit more," he said. "I'll wait for my pitch and try not to swing at so many bad pitches." Sammy took extra **batting practice** every day at Wrigley before games in the batting tunnel under the rightfield bleachers. Hitting coach Jeff Pentland would toss pitches in a high arc, making Sammy wait for them.

Meanwhile, St. Louis Cardinals hitter Mark McGwire was off to a flying start, too. He hit a grand slam on Opening Day and finished April with 11 homers. Then he got even hotter, blasting 18 more in May. He started June with 27 homers, more than twice as many as Sammy's 13. But Sammy homered in his first at bat of June and he homered in his last at bat of the month. In between, he hit 18 more, for a total of 20! No player in history hit more in a month. McGwire finished June with 37, with Sammy right behind at 33.

Sammy laughed and joked with reporters even when they asked silly questions like "Can you read English?" Sammy would read aloud from a newspaper and then ask the reporters if they could read Spanish. After interviews, he would shake hands with reporters and say "Gracias [thanks]." Sammy was gracious to everyone.

Sammy's 40th home run was a game-winning shot at Arizona, and it was his first grand slam. Before that, Sammy had had the most career home runs (247) without having ever hit a grand slam.

Sammy and Mark McGwire became friendly rivals in their home run race, which began in the 1998 season.

The very next day, Sammy hit another grand slam! He became the first Cub to hit grand slams in two straight days.

By mid-season, "The Great Home Run Race" had swept up everyone. Sammy and McGwire each had 47 homers when they finally met, face-to-face, on August 19 at Wrigley Field. Before the game, they hugged on the field.

"Maybe we'll go back to the Dominican Republic and retire together," Mac said to Sammy, "maybe build a golf club out there, call it Home Run Park."

In the fifth inning, Sammy drove a fastball from Kent Bottenfield out of leftfield for a three-run homer. He had taken the lead! Not for long, though. McGwire blasted No. 48 in the eighth inning, then smashed No. 49 in the 10th inning to win the game. Eleven days later in Colorado, Sammy blasted one 482 feet for his 54th, which tied McGwire again.

Sonia and Lucrecya Sosa help Sammy celebrate.

"This is Mark McGwire's show," Sammy said afterward. "I'm not going to steal his show. He's the man."

With three weeks left in the season, McGwire got hot. He smashed seven homers in seven days to reach 62. His record-breaker came against the Cubs. With Sammy four homers behind, he was asked if he felt any pressure to catch Big Mac.

"Pressure?" Sammy said, smiling. "Pressure is when you have to shine shoes and sell oranges just to make sure there's enough to eat at the next meal. When I was a shoeshine boy trying to make it to America, that was the real pressure."

In a three-game series at Wrigley against the Milwaukee Brewers, Sammy walloped four home runs to catch McGwire. The Cubs were locked in a three-team race for the league's wild-card spot with the Mets and Giants. Sammy belted a grand slam in San Diego to beat the Padres and help his team in the playoff race. In the home run race, Sammy had 63 homers, but McGwire had 65.

When the Cubs played their last home game of the 1998 season, they called it "Sammy Sosa Celebration Day." Chicago Bulls star Michael Jordan threw the first pitch. Sammy crouched behind the plate, and Jordan threw it ... way over Sammy's head.

A young ballplayer practices with a tennis ball in front of some of the destruction caused by Hurricane Georges in San Pedro de Macoris.

Baseball commissioner Bud Selig and Roger Maris's six children were there to honor Sammy. But most important to Sammy, his mother and his brothers were there.

Dominican flags and pennants with Sammy's name on them replaced the team pennants that usually fly above the outfield. Sammy received many gifts, including a maroon convertible car with the license plate *Sammy 98* and a crystal statue. With his family beaming, Sammy stepped to the microphone near home plate and thanked the commissioner, the coaches, the players, and the fans of Chicago. A special glow filled Sammy's face. He walked over to the stands to kiss his wife and mother. Then Sammy took a lap around the field, slapping high-fives with the fans and waving his cap. The day was perfect . . . until the Cubs lost, 7—3.

The Cubs finished up the season on the road. The team was in Milwaukee when Sammy heard some bad news. A devastating hurricane had swept through the Dominican Republic, killing people and destroying homes. Sammy's mother and brothers were with him. His sisters were safe, but the Sosas feared for their country. "It is bad," Sammy said. "Why does everything happen to my town and not to me?" That night he started the Sammy Sosa Charitable Foundation as a relief effort for all the Caribbean islands. Within days, more than $2 million poured into the foundation, much of the money coming from ballplayers.

When Sammy wasn't playing baseball, he helped load sacks of food onto trucks to be sent by plane to the islands. "This is something that is very important, something that I need to do for my country," he said. "It's a very tough situation back home, many people have lost their homes, and many people are hungry. The children don't have enough food and water, and they're scared because of everything that happened."

Sammy blasted home run No. 66 to pass McGwire with just three days left in the season. The next day, McGwire hit his 66th to tie Sammy, then McGwire smacked two more to take the lead. On the final day of the season, McGwire hit two more to reach 70. Sammy finished with 66.

The Cubs and Giants ended the season with identical records. The teams played a one-game playoff at Wrigley Field to determine the wild card winner. Sammy singled twice and scored two runs to lead the Cubs to a 5—3 victory. Chicago would play the Atlanta Braves in the National League playoffs. "This has just been a great year, a magical year," Sammy said. "If we win, that will be great, but if it doesn't happen, we'll still come back next year and try just as hard."

The Braves swept the Cubs in three games, and Sammy was on the next flight to the Dominican Republic. When he landed in his hometown, he saw mud-covered streets and houses turned into rubble.

Thousands of fans cheer as Sonia and Sammy Sosa parade through the streets of the Dominican Republic.

"Now that I am here," Sammy said, "I have time to go to every corner, to see what people need, what they really need."

Sammy went to New York for the first game of the 1998 World Series and threw out the first pitch. While he was in New York, the city honored him with a ticker-tape parade along a stretch of Broadway Avenue known as the Canyon of Heroes. Sammy was presented with the Roberto Clemente Humanitarian Award for his efforts. "This is a very, very, very, very nice country," he said. National TV networks wanted Sammy to be on their shows, but he said no. He wanted to get back home. "I want people to have their homes back. It is hard. I cannot do it all by myself, but I want to sacrifice myself."

After receiving an award for his humanitarian work, Sammy blows a kiss to the fans.

Back in San Pedro de Macoris, Sammy spent the next several months helping the people of his country rebuild their homes. In November, Sammy was named baseball's Most Valuable Player.

Sammy began his 1999 season in quiet fashion with just four homers in the first month of the season. But he picked up the pace, and by mid-season he had 37 home runs. In August, Sammy really got hot. He hit 18 home runs to end the month with 55, and on September 18, he became the first player in major league history to hit 60 homers twice.

"Last year, when I hit 62, Mark [McGwire] was already the first guy there," Sammy said. "This year, to be the first to reach 60, I have to say I enjoy this a little more."

McGwire had 56 home runs when Sammy hit his 60th. Neither player stopped blasting homers until the last game of the season. McGwire hit six home runs in the final seven games to catch and pass Sammy, who hit just three in the last two weeks.

Both the Cubs and the Cardinals had been eliminated from the postseason playoffs by the time the two teams met to close the 1999 regular season. In the final game, McGwire hit a home run—his 65th of the season—and Sammy hit a home run—his 63rd.

In 2001, Sammy nearly matched his awesome home run hitting pace of 1998.

Only four players in the history of major league baseball have ever hit more than 60 home runs, and McGwire and Sammy have done it twice!

In the 2000 and 2001 seasons, Sammy continued to show he was a force to be reckoned with. In 2001, during a game against the Cincinnati Reds, Sosa hit his 60th home run, becoming the first major-league player in history to have three 60-homer seasons.

"I am a happy man," said Sammy. "I had a great year. For me, that's something to be happy about."

Statistics

Minor League

Year	Level	Team	Games	At Bats	Runs	Hits	2B	3B	HR	RBI	Batting average
1986	Rookie	Sarasota	61	229	38	63	19	1	4	28	.275
1987	Class A	Gastonia	129	519	73	145	27	4	11	59	.279
1988	Class A	Port Charlotte	131	507	70	116	13	12	9	51	.229
1989	Class AA	Tulsa	66	273	45	81	15	4	7	31	.297
	Class AAA	Oklahoma City	10	39	2	4	2	0	0	3	.103
	Class AAA	Vancouver	13	49	7	18	3	0	1	5	.367
1991	Class AAA	Vancouver	32	116	19	31	7	2	3	19	.267
1992	Class AAA	Iowa#	5	19	3	6	2	0	0	1	.316

2B=doubles, 3B=triples, HR=home runs, RBI=runs batted in, BB=bases on balls (walks)
#Injury Rehabilitation Assignment

Major League

Year	Team	Games	At Bats	Runs	Hits	2B	3B	HR	RBI	Batting average
1989	Rangers	25	84	8	20	3	0	1	3	.238
	White Sox	33	99	19	27	5	0	3	10	.273
1990	White Sox	153	532	72	124	26	10	15	70	.233
1991	White Sox	116	316	39	64	10	1	10	33	.203
1992	Cubs	67	262	41	68	7	2	8	25	.260
1993	Cubs	159	598	92	156	25	5	33	93	.261
1994	Cubs	105	426	59	128	17	6	25	70	.300
1995	Cubs	144	564	89	151	17	3	36	119	.268
1996	Cubs	124	498	84	136	21	2	40	100	.273
1997	Cubs	162	642	90	161	31	4	36	119	.251
1998	Cubs	159	643	134	198	20	0	66	158	.308
1999	Cubs	162	625	114	180	24	2	63	141	.288
2000	Cubs	156	604	106	193	38	1	50	138	.320
2001	Cubs	160	577	146	189	34	5	64	160	.328
Totals		1,725	6,470	1,093	1,795	278	41	450	1,239	.277

Glossary

at bat: An official attempt to hit a pitched ball. Hitting a sacrifice, being walked, or being hit by a pitch doesn't count as an at bat.

batting average: The number of hits a batter gets, divided by the batter's official at bats, carried to three decimal places. For example, if Sammy gets 30 hits in 90 at bats, his batting average is .333.

batting practice: The time players spend before a game hitting pitches thrown by one of their own coaches.

bullpen: The relief pitchers (pitchers who don't start games).

count: The number of balls and strikes on a batter. The number of balls is always given first. For example, if the pitcher throws two balls to Sammy but the third pitch is a strike, the count is 2-and-1—two balls and one strike.

cutoff: The infielder who catches a throw from the outfielder and throws to another infielder to make a play. For example, if Sammy fields the ball deep in rightfield, he would throw to the second baseman—the cutoff—who would then throw to the catcher if a baserunner were heading for home.

grand slam: A home run hit when the bases are loaded. A grand slam scores four runs.

intentional walk: A deliberate walk—four balls thrown by the pitcher—to prevent a hitter from having a chance to drive in runs.

leadoff: The first batter in a lineup or an inning.

pitchout: An outside pitch that is thrown on purpose so that the catcher has a chance to throw out a runner.

run batted in (RBI): A run that is scored as a result of a hit or, if the bases are loaded, a walk.

sacrifice bunt: A play in which the batter is put out but the baserunner advances.

Sources

Information for this book was obtained from the following sources: Nancy Armour (*Associated Press*, 20 September 1998); Michael Bamberger (*Sports Illustrated*, 28 September 1998); Chicago Cubs Media Guide (1998); Ken Daley (*Dallas Morning News*, 23 September 1998); Bill Fleischman (*New York Daily News*, 23 September 1998); Toni Ginnetti (*Baseball Digest*, September 1998); Tom Haudricourt (*Milwaukee Journal Sentinel*, 22 September 1998); Jon Heyman (*Newsday*, 23 September 1998); Charles Hirshberg (*Life*, January 1999); Richard Jerome (*People*, 28 September 1998); John Lowe (*Detroit Free Press*, 30 September 1998); Bill Plaschke (*Los Angeles Times*, 23 September 1998); Ken Rosenthal (*Baltimore Sun*, 24 September 1998); Steve Rushin (*Sports Illustrated*, 14 September 1998); Gary Smith (*Sports Illustrated*, 21 December 1998); Jayson Stark (*Philadelphia Inquirer*, 20 September 1998); David Steele (*San Francisco Chronicle*, 26 September 1998); Joel Stein (*Time*, 28 September 1998); Paul Sullivan (*Chicago Tribune*, 15 September 1998; 18 October 1998; 4 October 1999); Tom Verducci (*Sports Illustrated*, 29 June 1998).

Index

Write to Sammy:

You can send mail to Sammy at the address on the right. If you write a letter, don't get your hopes up too high. Sammy and other athletes get lots of letters every day, and they aren't always able to answer them all.

Sammy Sosa
c/o Chicago Cubs
Wrigley Field
1060 West Addison Street
Chicago, IL 60613-4397

Acknowledgments

Photographs are reproduced with permission of: © Reuters/Mike Blake/Archive Photos, pp. 1, 13, 49; © Tim Broekma/ALLSPORT USA, pp. 2–3; © Vincent LaForet/ALLSPORT USA, p. 6; © Reuters/Jeff Christensen/Archive Photos, p. 9; © Jonathan Daniel/ALLSPORT USA, pp. 11, 26, 31, 33; © Reuters/Scott Olson/Archive Photos, p. 15; © Larry Jenkins/Good Luck Photography, pp. 16, 41; © CORBIS/Bettmann, p. 21; © Reuters/Onorio Montas/Archive Photos, p. 25; © CORBIS/AFP, p. 34; © John Swart/ALLSPORT USA, p. 36; © Jeff Carlick/ENDZONE, p. 42; © CORBIS/Matt Mendelsohn, p. 44; © ALLSPORT USA, p. 46; © Reuters/Sue Ogrocki/Archive Photos, p. 50; © AP/Wide World Photos, p. 52; © Reuters/Carole Devillers/Archive Photos, p. 55; © Reuters/Mike Segar/Archive Photos, p. 56; © Jonathan Kirn/SportsChrome East/West, p. 58.

Front cover photograph by © Jonathan Daniel/ALLSPORT USA. Back cover photograph by © AP/Wide World Photos.

About the Author

Jeff Savage is the author of more than 80 sports books for young readers, including LernerSports biographies of Julie Foudy, Tiger Woods, and Mark McGwire.